NATIONAL GEOGRAPHIC KiDS

W9-AWZ-227

EVERYTHING
DOGS

NATIONAL GEOGRAPHIC
KiDS

EVERYTHING DOGS

BECKY BAINES

WITH DR. GARY WEITZMAN

NATIONAL GEOGRAPHIC
WASHINGTON, D.C.

CONTENTS

A beagle, a Labrador, and a Brittany spaniel hang out together at a dog park. Because their ancestors were pack animals, many dogs love playtime with their pals.

INTRODUCTION

AH, DOGS. THE ULTIMATE PET.

They'll lick your face if you've had a bad day. They'll do silly stunts to make you laugh. They're loyal allies through thick and thin. No wonder they're called "man's best friend."

But did you know there's so much more to dogs than chasing a ball or fetching a stick? That's right! Underneath that furry, slobbery exterior is more than 15,000 years of fascinating history that made dogs the complex critters they are today. The only animals on Earth whose appearance and behavior have been carefully crafted by humans—puppy dogs are not just cuddly and cute, they really did change the face of the world.

From their ancient beginnings to wild canine cousins, super senses and incredible instincts, it's no wonder these pets are top dog. With up to 400 breeds—each unique and different—let's find out EVERYTHING about DOGS!

EXPLORER'S CORNER

Hi! I'm Dr. Gary Weitzman, and I'm a veterinarian. For the past ten years I've been lucky enough to run a big animal shelter called the Washington Animal Rescue League. We take in about 2,000 cats and dogs each year. We clean them up and make them healthy, so they can be adopted by families. I'll kind of be like a tour guide on your journey through this book. Every time you see this Explorer's Corner, look for me to give you bonus information!

A border collie runs through a flowery field. Perked up ears and tail means it's playtime for this pup!

Dogs come in all sorts of shapes and sizes. It's hard to believe they all came from the same ancestor!

1
MEET THE DOGS

CANINE 101

BEFORE WE DIVE
INTO THE WONDERFUL
WORLD OF WAGGING TAILS
and squeaky toys, we need to answer
a few things up front. The first
question is . . .

WHAT IS A DOG?

Well, that's easy . . . a dog is an adorable
bundle of fur that greets you at the front door
when you get home from school, and occasionally drinks out of the toilet. Right? Eh, not so
simple. The truth of the matter is that "dog" is
a generic term for a whole family of animals
called Canidae. Many animals besides man's
best friend are in this family. That wolf you see
howling on TV? Dog. That fox hiding behind
the trash cans? Dog. That coyote wandering
through the prairie? Dog. That prairie dog
popping out of the ground? Okay, that's not a
dog . . . but you see where this is going.

Members of the dog family share a few
common characteristics: They are mostly
predators, and they have teeth and jaws
suited for catching prey. Many are social
animals, meaning that in the wild, they live in
groups. The majority of Canidae also have long
bodies with similar structures that help them
run and catch their meals. Which leads us to
our second question . . .

WHAT KIND OF DOG IS THIS BOOK ABOUT?

We will get a little more in depth about a dog's extended family later. But for the most part, this book is about domestic dogs—aka your furry pal who occasionally drinks out of the toilet. Domestic dogs are quite a unique group of animals. What sets them apart? Their history with humans. In fact, the word *domestic* in this sense means "tamed by humans." That's because your fuzzy Fido is really just a wolf in dog's clothing. For the full history of dogs, you can flip to chapter 3, but here's what you need to know for now.

Scientists believe that thousands of years ago, humans domesticated (tamed) the gray wolf to help them with work around the farm, and for protection against unwanted visitors (such as bears, wild boar, or lions—depending on where they lived). Over time, humans bred wolves—put them together with a mate for the purpose of having babies—to have characteristics that they wanted in the dogs: better hunters, better watchdogs, smaller, bigger, and so on. When they did this over and over, the dogs began to look very different from their wolf-y roots, and very different from each other. That's how modern breeds of domestic dogs came to be. Today, there are 350 to 400 breeds of domesticated dog.

By the Numbers

78.2 MILLION
The number of dogs owned in the United States in 2011

118
The number of dogs owned by U.S. Presidents while they were in office

#1
The ranking of the Labrador retriever on the American Kennel Club's 2011 list of most popular dog breeds

22
The number of consecutive years the poodle was the most popular breed

21
The number of U.S. colleges and universities that have bulldogs as mascots

TOP BIG DOGS

IT MAY BE HARD TO BELIEVE THAT an animal that started as a gray wolf evolved into hundreds of different breeds . . . or that a 150-pound (68 kg) English mastiff is even related to a 4-pound (1.8 kg) Chihuahua. But it's true! With so many shapes and sizes to pick from, it's impossible to cover them all. Let's take a look at the furry facts behind some of the most popular big dogs.

NAME: **LABRADOR RETRIEVER**
NICKNAME: Black Lab, Yellow Lab, Chocolate Lab
COUNTRY OF ORIGIN: Canada (in Newfoundland)
BEST KNOWN FOR: Athletic ability, intelligence, great swimming ability

Labradors are excellent runners and swimmers. They were originally bred to retrieve fishing nets off the sides of boats in the Labrador Sea. That's how they got their name! Their smart, friendly nature and gentle demeanor make them the most popular service dog.

NAME: **ENGLISH BULLDOG**
NICKNAME: Bully
COUNTRY OF ORIGIN: England, U.K.
BEST KNOWN FOR: Pushed-in face, wrinkly nose, stocky build

This flat-faced, squishy dog is perhaps one of the most well-known and lovable breeds, but it has a surprisingly sad history. It was originally bred in England to fight bulls, which is how it got its name. Luckily, the fights were outlawed in 1885, and bulldogs became the charming pets they are today.

NAME: **GOLDEN RETRIEVER**
NICKNAME: Yellow Retriever, Goldie
COUNTRY OF ORIGIN: Scotland, U.K.
BEST KNOWN FOR: Swimming, cuddling, tricks

One of the most popular breeds of dogs, goldies make great pets. These fun-loving, full-of-energy pups are loyal and easy to train, and if you lose a flip-flop in the ocean, a goldie will bring it back! That's because they were originally bred to retrieve ducks from the water.

NAME: GERMAN SHEPHERD
NICKNAME: K-9 Cop
COUNTRY OF ORIGIN: Germany
BEST KNOWN FOR: Police service, sharply pointed ears, obedience

Originally bred by a German military captain for service during wartime, German shepherds have gained notoriety over the years as police dogs. But despite their appearance, these pups are loyal and friendly, and big softies at heart.

NAME: BOXER
NICKNAME: n/a
COUNTRY OF ORIGIN: Germany
BEST KNOWN FOR: Funny faces, playful attitude, lovable personalities

Boxers are the clowns among canines. Aptly named for their tendency to box, that is, get up on their rear legs and bat around their "opponents," these athletic dogs are well known for their playful attitudes, silly mannerisms, and the longest tongue of any breed.

Bernese mountain dogs were built to work and are happiest when they have a job to do. Originally bred in the Swiss mountains as draft dogs, or dogs that pull a cart, these gentle giants can pull up to five times their weight!

NAME: BERNESE MOUNTAIN DOG
NICKNAME: Berner
COUNTRY OF ORIGIN: Switzerland
BEST KNOWN FOR: Large stature, strong build, shaggy coat, lovable nature

BIG DOG RECORD BREAKERS!
From colossal canines to a high-flying hound, check out these big dog superstars!

THE BIGGEST:
ZORBA THE ENGLISH MASTIFF

At 8.3 feet (2.5 m) long and 343 pounds (155.6 kg), Zorba holds the Guinness World Record for the largest dog ever recorded. He passed away at the age of eight in 1989, but his record remains intact.

THE TALLEST:
GIANT GEORGE THE GREAT DANE

At 7.3 feet (2.2 m) tip to tail and 42.6 inches (1.1 m) tall, Giant George is the tallest dog ever recorded. He weighs 245 pounds (111.1 kg), about 100 pounds (45.4 kg) more than the average Great Dane.

HIGHEST JUMPER:
CINDERELLA THE GREYHOUND

Jumping an incredible 68 inches (1.7 m), Cinderella the greyhound, also known as Soaring Cindy, broke her own record three times to create the new standard for the world's highest jumping dog.

PAW PRINT THERE ARE MORE PET DOGS IN THE WORLD—ABOUT HALF A BILLION—THAN HUMAN BABIES.

TOP SMALL DOGS

When it comes to cute and cuddly, westies have it covered. Fast and feisty? They're that too! Born hunters, westies originated in Scotland, where they kept away unwanted pests. Famously fearless and darn good diggers, these lapdogs will keep you on your toes!

NAME: WEST HIGHLAND WHITE TERRIER
NICKNAME: Westie
COUNTRY OF ORIGIN: Scotland, U.K.
BEST KNOWN FOR: Bright white coat, furry face, spunky attitude

BIG DOGS MIGHT MAKE

GREAT PILLOWS, BUT SOMETIMES THERE'S nothing better than a furry little fella who can curl up in your lap. These guys are small, but many of them can still run with the big dogs. Read on to discover the tail-wagging truth about some of the most popular small breeds.

NAME: PEMBROKE WELSH CORGI
NICKNAME: Corgi
COUNTRY OF ORIGIN: Wales, U.K.
BEST KNOWN FOR: Big ears, long bodies, frisky nature

Dachshunds may look silly with their long "hot dog" bodies, but they were built with a purpose. In their native Germany, *dachs* means "badger," and *hund* means "hound." That's right—dachshunds are badger hounds! Their long, thin shape once helped them squeeze through under-ground tunnels.

Now here's a dog fit for royalty. Queen Elizabeth II is said to be such a fan of the corgi, they actually appear with her in a royal portrait. You can't blame her. With their long, shaggy bodies; short, stubby legs; and bat-like ears—corgis are adorable!

NAME: DACHSHUND
NICKNAME: Hot Dogs, Wiener Dogs
COUNTRY OF ORIGIN: Germany
BEST KNOWN FOR: Long bodies, stubby legs

NAME: JACK RUSSELL TERRIER
NICKNAME: Parson Russell Terrier, Jack
COUNTRY OF ORIGIN: United Kingdom
BEST KNOWN FOR: Excitable nature, high-jumping, athletic ability

MICRO MUTTS!
Here are three puny pups for the record books!

THE SMALLEST (HEIGHT):
BOO BOO THE CHIHUAHUA

At a teeny four inches tall (10.2 cm), Boo Boo was declared the smallest dog in the world (in terms of height) in 2007.

THE SMALLEST (LENGTH):
BRANDY THE CHIHUAHUA

Measuring six inches (15.2 cm) from the tip of her nose to the tip of her tail, Heaven Sent Brandy was proclaimed the smallest living dog (in terms of length) in 2005.

THE LIGHTEST:
DANCER THE CHIHUAHUA

Weighing in at a mere 1.2 pounds (0.5 kg), Dancer is the world's lightest dog.

If you're looking for a nice quiet lapdog, you are not looking for a Jack Russell terrier. These crazy canines yip, yap, bark, and run, and they can jump five times their own height. Super speedy and independent, Jacks were originally bred for fox hunting and need plenty of room to run.

NAME: PUG
NICKNAME: n/a
COUNTRY OF ORIGIN: China
BEST KNOWN FOR: Flat face, wrinkles, bug eyes, curly tail

With a short, flat face, deep-set wrinkles, and bug eyes, pugs were originally the pet of choice for Buddhist monks in Tibet. Rumored to have been bred to bear the mark of "the prince," the Chinese characters for that word appear in the wrinkles on a pug's forehead.

With their soft, fluffy hair and a style all their own, poodles appear to be the most sophisticated dogs around. But that hair once served an important purpose. The poodle—the word comes from the German word for puddle—is actually a water dog, and its hair was intended to keep its joints warm.

NAME: TOY POODLE
NICKNAME: n/a
COUNTRY OF ORIGIN: Countries in Northern Europe
BEST KNOWN FOR: Intelligence, tricks, signature haircut

PAW PRINT IF HUMANS VARIED IN SIZE AS MUCH AS DOGS, THE SMALLEST WOULD BE 2 FEET (0.6 M) AND THE TALLEST UP TO 31 FEET (9.4 M).

INCREDIBLE INSTINCTS

IMAGINE LIFE WITH **NO VIDEO GAMES, SOCCER PRACTICE,** or sleepovers. Pretty boring right? Not for your dog! He's totally happy just eating, sleeping, and chasing the same ball over and over . . . but what's up with burying bones in the couch? Did you know there are very good reasons why dogs do the things they do? What seems silly, cute, or funny to us is built-in instinct for them. See for yourself, dogs are born for this stuff!

WHY DO DOGS LIKE TO FETCH?

While scientists don't know for certain why dogs like to fetch, many agree that there are two reasons:

1. Dogs don't have great eyesight, but nature makes up for it by giving them good peripheral vision—that is, at any one time they can see more of the space around them than we can. In the wild, wolves scan their surroundings from a still position. They are alerted to prey when they notice an object moving at a fast speed. That's when instinct kicks in, and they chase it.

2. Wolves are social animals, and when they kill something they bring it back to share with the rest of the pack. When you throw a ball it might trigger this same response in your dog. That's why your furry friend chases it, retrieves it, and then brings it back to share with you. How thoughtful!

WHY DO DOGS HIDE BONES?

Believe it or not, the instinct to bury or stash food isn't dog-specific—it's pretty common in the animal kingdom. Many species, from crocodiles to cheetahs to squirrels, have a hankering to hide.

This is true because in the wild, animals can't pop through a drive-through if they're hungry. They have to work hard for their meals. Sometimes finding food is easy, but sometimes it's not. They have to be smart to survive. So when food is available, many animals hide it to save for a rainy day. Your pup may not have to worry about this, but its wolf ancestors did, and that instinct stuck around.

WHY DO DOGS ROLL IN SMELLY STUFF?

There are two popular theories behind why dogs go out for a romp in the yard, and come back smelling like last night's tuna noodle casserole if it had sat out in the sun for a week. The first is that wild dogs, who use their sense of smell to communicate with one another, are not only hunters but also scavengers. Meaning, if they find something dead that's still edible, they'll dig in. Some scientists believe that if they stumble across an animal carcass, they'll roll in it to pick up the smell, and bring that back to the other pack members to let them know what they've found.

The second possibility is that wolves passed on to their doggy cousins the stealth plan to use the stinky stuff to disguise their own scent. That way, other animals can't smell a predator coming and take off like a rocket before they become dinner.

Both theories are equally possible, and equally gross.

WHY DO DOGS BARK

Your dog's constant barking got you down? This is one furry feature you can't blame on their wolf-y ancestors. But you can blame your human ones! That's right—new research shows that the tendency to bark loudly, repeatedly, and often annoyingly was intentionally bred into dogs by people.

Wolves are not quiet animals: They whine, whimper, growl, and howl, but they usually don't bark. That's because it's not in their nature. When people first began domesticating dogs, scientists think they bred them to bark. Why? To be the world's first home alarm system, of course. So next time your dad gets mad at your dog for barking at the mail carrier, remind him that if it was a burglar he would feel very differently.

EXPLORER'S CORNER

Many people wonder why some dogs bite. It's not because they're mean, it's all about communication. Dogs bite when they feel threatened or scared. But the act of biting is actually the last step in the process. Most dogs exhibit other behaviors before they snap, such as rigid body posture, tilting of the head, baring of teeth, possible growling, and then, finally, biting. It's their way of saying "back off!" The best way to avoid being bitten is to always ask the owner if it's okay to approach their pup. No one knows a dog's personality better than its human.

A PHOTOGRAPHIC DIAGRAM

A CLOSER LOOK AT CANINES

MAN'S BEST FRIEND MAY BE

A SWEET LITTLE PUPPY DOG NOW, BUT THANKS TO ITS WILD HISTORY, IT'S STILL BUILT LIKE A beast. The recipe may have changed, but the canine ingredients remain the same. Take a look at the features that make your furry friend a powerful predator.

TAIL

A dog's tail is very important for communication. The position and movement of the tail mean different things, which, for their wolf cousins, is crucial for survival.

MUSCLES

Dogs have well-defined muscles, especially in the front and back legs, that allow them to run like the wind and leap like a leopard to catch a meal.

LEGS

While a dog's front legs are fairly flexible, the back legs are sturdy and powerful to allow them to burst into speed from a standing start.

COAT

Dogs' coats vary as widely as the breeds themselves. Water dogs have oily coats. Working dogs have double coats. Poodles have hair instead of fur. Mexican hairless dogs have no coats. Coats can be long or short, coarse or soft. They can be red, yellow, white, black, or brown, and have any number of patterns.

TONGUE
A dog's tongue is helpful in regulating body temperature. Dogs pant when they are overheated to move cooler air over their tongue into their bodies.

EARS
A dog's ears come in four different styles: pricked (upright), dropped (hangs down), button (folds over), and cropped (surgically altered).

EYES
Dogs' eyes are dichromatic, which means they can see variations of blue and yellow. Their sense of vision is dull compared to ours, but their field of vision is wider and they have better night vision.

TEETH
Dogs have 42 teeth—perfect for catching prey, and ripping, pulling, tearing, and shredding meat.

PAWS
Dog paws are small, which allows them to change direction quickly mid-sprint. They have four claws and often a fifth claw farther up their leg—a dewclaw, used for gripping.

FRONT LEGS
Dogs don't have a collarbone like humans do. Their front legs are only attached by muscle, which allows them a longer stride while running.

MUZZLE
Dog breeds have skulls and muzzles that are short (pug), medium (Dalmatian), or long (greyhound). Research shows that dogs with short muzzles are better able to see single objects, and dogs with long muzzles see more of their surroundings.

2

A DOG'S LIFE

A Dalmatian weaves in and out of poles in an agility competition. Agility competitions test a dog's ability to follow commands.

PUPPY PAUSE

AWWWW! IS THERE ANYTHING CUTER THAN A SOFT, fluffy, big-eyed, bouncy, tail-wagging little puppy? Probably not. In fact, puppies are so adorable that studies show they may actually relieve stress in humans. There is a new trend called puppy therapy, in which dog rescue organizations bring puppies to college students studying for exams to help relieve stress. Does it work? Maybe. Regardless, it beats a pop quiz any day! And if one puppy is cute, how about five? Or six? Or seven?

LEAPING LITTERS!

Puppies are born in litters that typically range from two to ten puppies, though there may be only one, or as many as 24! Large dogs usually have bigger litters than small dogs.

NEEDY NEWBORNS!

Puppies are born with a fully developed sense of smell, but they are blind and not able to keep warm on their own. Because of this they are fully dependent on mom for the first few weeks of life, relying on smell to find her. They begin to nurse as soon as they are born and clump into one big puppy pile to sleep and keep warm.

PLAYFUL PUPS!

At around nine to eleven days old, pups open their eyes and get their first peek at their puppy playmates. Around this time their ears also open, and they are much more likely to respond to sound. Between two and four weeks old, puppies start to do what puppies do best—growl, bark, bite, roll around, and play with their brothers and sisters.

At about one month old, puppies generally start eating solid food and stop relying on mom so much, though they should stay with the litter for a few more weeks before they are adopted by new families.

WILD CHILD

Wolf pups are born in a den, a hole or cave that their mom found or dug before they were born. At birth, they are actually very similar to domestic puppies. They are completely blind and reliant on mom for everything. The difference starts at about three weeks old, when they begin to eat meat. Wolf pups are raised by the whole pack. Older siblings babysit while the rest of the pack goes on a hunt. Wolf pups can't hunt until they are about six months old, so adult wolves eat as much as they can and bring it back in their stomachs. The pups lick around their parents' mouths, and mom or dad sends the food up and out into the pups' mouths. Yuck!

EXPLORER'S CORNER

The first three months of a puppy's life are crucial. This is the period when they absorb the most information about the world around them, so you want to expose puppies to every new experience you can. Some good examples might be loud noises and unfamiliar objects. If a dog is sheltered from normal experiences early in life, it might be skittish or afraid of everyday things as it gets older.

PAW PRINT ALL DOGS ARE CONSIDERED PUPPIES FOR THEIR FIRST TWO YEARS OF LIFE.

DOG DAYS

9:00 A.M.

1:10 P.M.

EVER WONDERED WHAT
YOUR DOG IS DOING WHILE YOU'RE AT
school? The answer is probably more boring than you think, because dogs sleep a *lot*. But who knows? Not every dog is the same . . . maybe yours invites the neighborhood mutts over for a poker game. But if your furry friend kept a diary, here's what it would likely say:

7:30 A.M. Woke up short male and female humans in usual way. Licked female's face.

8:00 A.M. Strolled around backyard. Pee smells are exactly where I left them.

8:15 A.M. Dog food again for breakfast. Cleaned bowl in three gobbles.

9:00 A.M. Rode with small humans to school. Best smells come when window is open.

9:30 A.M. Back home. Favorite spot in sun was open. Napped. Dreamed about running and barking.

NOON Went for walk with tall female human who drives the car and feeds me. Discovered new pee scent a few blocks down.

1:05 P.M. Rewarded with milk bone for "doing good business." Must find out what this means. Hid bone in couch to enjoy later.

CANINE CUISINE

If you've ever come home to a knocked-over trash can with banana peels and moldy bread full of teeth marks and paw prints, you know that dogs are not the pickiest of eaters. This might be because they have about one-fifth the taste buds that humans have, but there's another reasonable explanation. Sure, dogs are carnivores by nature and, therefore, have a mind for meat, but they're also scavengers and are genetically encoded to eat what they can find. What may be trash to you makes perfectly good leftovers to them. But some foods that are harmless to humans can be deadly for dogs. Here are some things you should never feed Fido:

- ☠ **CHOCOLATE**
- ☠ **GRAPES OR RAISINS**
- ☠ **MACADAMIA NUTS**
- ☠ **MUSHROOMS**
- ☠ **ONIONS OR GARLIC**
- ☠ **PERSIMMONS**
- ☠ **RAW EGGS**
- ☠ **RAW MEAT**
- ☠ **RHUBARB**
- ☠ **SUGAR-FREE CANDY**

4:15 P.M.

1:10 P.M. Napped. Dreamed I ran and barked.

4:00 P.M. Woke to find short humans home. Too many new smells on both of them to count.

4:15 P.M. Walked to park with short male human. Hit in head by Frisbee. Rocky, the squirrel, outran me again. Human did not want dirty tennis ball I found for him.

5:15 P.M. Lucked out again—dog food for dinner.

5:30 P.M. TV time. Short female human used me for pillow after tall male used me for footstool.

6:30 P.M. Human dinner time. Lay under table until tall male ordered me out of kitchen. Snuck back under table.

8:30 P.M. Routine evening backyard patrol revealed new cat scents. We don't have a cat. Covered scents best I could with my own.

9:00 P.M. Bedtime. Warmed tall humans' bed for them. Pushed off.

9:03 P.M. Warmed short female's bed. Pushed off.

9:07 P.M. Warmed short male's bed. Pushed off.

9:09 P.M. Paced house. Ate a spider. Couldn't find milk bone in couch.

9:38 P.M. Slept with head under bed. Note to self: Find bone tomorrow.

PEE MARKS THE SPOT

Why does your dog take so many bathroom breaks on a walk? No, you didn't over-water him. It's all about the nose. The sense of smell is super important in the canine world. It tells dogs just about all they need to know about everything and everyone. For a dog, pee is about as information-packed as your computer's hard drive. When a dog smells another dog's pee, it's like reading their Dogbook page. So, why does your pup potty on everything? The number one rule for all dogs (wild and domestic) is to establish territory and protect it. By peeing on that fence, your pup is saying, "This is mine."

BEND IT LIKE A BORDER COLLIE

FOR THOUSANDS OF YEARS, BEFORE THE MODERN CONVENIENCES OF CARS, HOME SECURITY

systems, and MP3 players, dogs had a hand in helping humans cope with the day-to-day stress of life. They tended fields, watched sheep, and ate rodents. Now that most dogs have the cushy job of sleeping all day and occasionally scratching, how are they to satisfy the need to run, play, and please their humans? The answer is . . . professional doggie sports!

FLYBALL

Flyball is a canine supersport that can be best described as a relay race, with tennis, hurdles, and a little bowling thrown in. It's a team sport for all those pups who like to share in the glory, and the object is simple: Run down a course, retrieve the tennis ball, run back. It gets a little tricky when you throw in the fact that each dog is running head-to-head against another dog over four hurdles down each lane. To retrieve the tennis ball, the dog has to step on a lever that sends it soaring through the air and then catch it while running 30 miles an hour (48.2 km/h) . . . but you know . . . what dog can't do that?

PAW PRINT NOT INTO THE SUPERBOWL? NO WORRIES! ON GAME DAY, CHECK YOUR CABLE LISTINGS TO WATCH THE PUPPYBOWL INSTEAD—THREE HOURS OF PUPPIES FROM LOCAL SHELTERS ROLLING AROUND IN A MINIATURE STADIUM.

DISC DOG

Here's a sport for all your fun-loving fetchers out there. In the intense competition of disc dog, you throw a disc and your dog catches it—kind of like you would if you were playing Frisbee. But to make it a little more of a challenge, the dog stands at your feet while you throw the disc. Then they run to catch it while it's still in the air. Not impressed? The world record is 317 feet (96.6 m)! The other type of disc dog—freestyle—is more like a choreographed dance routine between you and your dog. You earn points with tricks and creativity. Popular moves include the dog catching the disc by jumping off its owner's back, and weaving in between its owner's legs. Maybe you shouldn't try this one if your dog weighs more than you.

EARTHDOG

Sure, Earthdog might *sound* like a peaceful superhero who uses the forces of nature to combat his enemies, but it is a game designed for small breed dogs such as westies and dachshunds that were originally bred to chase small prey through narrow tunnels underground. In Earthdog competitions, a course is built using a series of wooden boxes, and the dogs must follow a series of twists and turns chasing the scent of a rat. Proud pups can win the title Master Earthdog! Ruler of All Things!

Record Numbers

5 The most tennis balls a dog has ever held in its mouth at one time

6 The most consecutive items caught by a dog in competition

13 The most dogs skipping on the same rope at one time

16 The most Frisbees caught by a dog in three minutes

18,113 The number of dog participants in the largest dog walk ever held

AGILITY

Dog agility is the ultimate competition for bragging rights between dog and owner. If your pup wants to prove it's the most well-trained hound in the hood, agility is where it's at. That's because no two agility events are exactly the same—it's an obstacle course that changes every time, so part of the warm-up is familiarizing your dog with the lay of the land. The obstacles change as well, but they generally include tunnels, seesaws, ramps, weaving poles, and jumps. To master agility your dog must be an obedience expert, because there is no touching allowed. Participants must guide their dogs using only signals and voice commands.

DECODING DOGS

YOU MIGHT THINK THAT IF YOU WANT A TALKING PET, **YOU HAVE TO BUY A BIRD—OR ONE OF THOSE WEIRD DOGS ON THE INTERNET** that can bark "I love you." But as it turns out, your dog probably talks to you all the time! You just need to learn how to listen. Check out the chart below to understand the doggie dictionary.

DOGGIE DEMEANOR	EARS	MOUTH	BODY	TELL TAIL	HOUND SOUND
ALERT	Perked up, turning to catch sounds	Closed or open slightly but not showing teeth	Normal or on tiptoe	Up or wagging	No sound, low whine, or alarm bark
ANXIOUS	Partially back	Closed or slightly open "grinning"	Slightly lowered	Slightly lowered	Low whine or moaning bark
CURIOUS/ EXCITED	Perked up, maybe slightly forward	Open or closed, no teeth showing, possibly panting	Wiggling, standing on tiptoe, pacing	Up, wagging	Short, excited barks, whining
AGGRESSIVE	Forward or back, close to head	Drawn back to expose teeth	Tense, upright	Straight out from body or fluffed up	Growl, snarl, bark
DOMINANT	Up straight or forward	Open or closed, no teeth showing	Standing very tall	Stiffened and fluffed	Low assertive growl or grunt
SCARED	Laid back flat or low on head	Drawn back to expose teeth, or closed	Tense, crouched low, shivering, trembling	Tucked between legs	Low worried yelp, whine, or growl
FRIENDLY	Up, alert	Open, relaxed, possibly "smiling"	Normal, still, or wiggling butt	Wagging	Whimpering, yapping, short, high bark
THREATENED	Perked up, forward	Baring teeth	Tense, rigid	Straight out and fluffed up	Low growl, loud alert barking
PLAYFUL/ HAPPY	Perked up and forward or relaxed	Relaxed and open, "smiling"	Wiggling, excited bouncing, circling, may bow with rear in air	Wagging excitedly	Excited bark, low play growl
SHAMED/ SUBMISSIVE	Down, flattened back against head	Lips pulled back in a grin	Crouched low to ground, head down, or rolled over on back to reveal tummy	Tucked between legs	Whine, whimper

GO FETCH . . . ME A SODA

Believe it or not, you can actually train a dog to open a refrigerator and retrieve whatever you want. The trick is to tie a dishrag or rope to the handle so the dog can open it by tugging. Keep in mind this means pup can come and go as he pleases, so you run the risk of losing anything you left on that bottom shelf. Quick, save the cheesecake!

CLEVER CANINES

Understanding canine communication is important to knowing your dog's wants and needs. Then again, if you teach your pup a few of these tricks, it might make life a lot easier for him (and you)!

GIVE ME A RING!

Sure, your dog has probably learned to sit in front of the door if he needs to go out. But what if you're not nearby to notice? There's a very good chance you could be scrubbing carpets. Teaching Rover to ring a bell is actually very simple. Hang a bell from the doorknob of the door you usually use to take him out. Every time you let him out, ring the bell. Pretty soon, your pup will associate the bell with the door opening, and ring it himself!

DON'T FORGET TO FLUSH!

You won't need a bell if you can pull off this last trick: teaching your dog to use a toilet. That's right, it's possible! It's also pretty complicated, so you'll probably want to look up the actual instructions, which are widely available on the Internet. Let's just say this one might take a while. Also—best to ask mom and dad before you attempt it. They might be really confused when they go to take their morning shower and find Brutus doing his business.

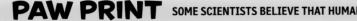

PAW PRINT SOME SCIENTISTS BELIEVE THAT HUMANS AND DOGS ARE SO IN TUNE, DOGS CAN ACTUALLY UNDERSTAND HUMAN EMOTIONS.

A PHOTO GALLERY

DIVERSE DOGGIES

YOU MIGHT WONDER WHY THE NUMBER OF DOG BREEDS

in the world ranges from about 350 to 400. That's because it's not a scientifically classified categorization. Dog breeds are identified by kennel clubs and canine organizations. Different groups might list slightly different breeds, so the actual number is unclear. But whether a dog is considered a specific breed or not, they sure are pretty darn cute!

Afghan hounds all but disappeared during World War I, but made a comeback in the 1920s.

Weimaraners are thought to have been bred from bloodhounds, which made them perfect hunting dogs.

Pitbull breeds often get a bad rap and are labeled aggressive, when in fact they make excellent service dogs.

Dobermans are great guard dogs—very intelligent and good at following commands.

Boxers are very funny, incredibly athletic, and always full of energy.

Irish setters are a high-energy breed with fun personalities.

Labradoodles are a mix of a Labrador retriever and a poodle, both of which are water-lovin' dogs.

Like all puppies, these beagle babies are huddling together for warmth. Most beagles have a distinct tricolor coat.

With their stubby legs and long "hot dog" bodies, dachshunds always steal the show.

The original shaggy dogs, bearded collies are very popular in the agility circuit.

3

WE ARE FAMILY

The ancestors of domestic dogs—gray wolves—are fast and fierce hunters. These wolves leap over a fallen tree in search of their next meal.

DOG FAMILY TREE

THE HISTORY OF DOMESTIC DOGS IS A BIT FUZZY, BUT ONE THING'S

for sure: If every member of the dog family got together for a family reunion, it would be a *big* event.

As you learned in Canine 101, domestic dogs are members of the family Canidae, of which 39 species still exist. Other cunning Canidae include wild dogs, wolves, foxes, jackals, coyotes, and dingoes. They all have one common ancestor called *Eucyon Davisi,* which was a giant king of dogs, much larger than the gray wolf is today. Somewhere along the way, *Eucyon Davisi* split into two separate lines and continued to evolve into different species of canidae, including the family canini, or "true dogs," and vulpini, which includes all species of fox. Most members of the family Canidae have very similar characteristics, but each with its own strengths. Check out these doggie distinctions.

JACKAL

BEST LONG-DISTANCE RUNNER
All dogs are fast, but when it comes to long-distance running, nothing beats a jackal. Jackals can sprint up to 35 miles an hour (56.3 kph), and they can maintain at least 16 miles an hour (25.7 kph) over very long distances.

WILD DOG

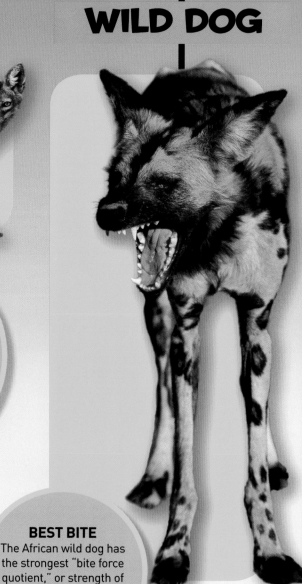

BEST BITE
The African wild dog has the strongest "bite force quotient," or strength of bite relative to weight, of any mammal in the world.

PAW PRINT AUSTRALIAN CATTLE DOGS ARE PART DINGO.

EUCYON DAVISI

TRUE DOGS
(canini)

FOX
(vulpini)

MOST INDIVIDUAL
Because they are in a different lineage than true dogs, foxes have characteristics that set them apart. They are smaller, and have sharper, pointy snouts. They're omnivorous, which means they eat both meat and veggies, and they generally don't live in packs.

WOLF

DINGO

COYOTE

BEST HUNTER
Wolves are not only the biggest canines, they are also the best at catching a meal. Wolves hunt in packs of up to ten, and can roam 30 miles a day (48 km) looking for prey. When they find it, they can sprint up to 40 miles an hour (64.4 kph) from a standing start, and grab their target with their sharp, interlocking teeth that stop it from getting away.

BEST PET RUNNER-UP
Although illegal in many places, it is understood that if a dingo is taken from the litter when it's young enough it can be raised as a domestic dog. Some people even argue that it should be considered a domestic dog breed. But wild dingoes can be very dangerous, so don't go setting dingo traps in your backyard.

SMARTEST
Sure, your pet dog can lie down and roll over, but will it watch its next meal for hours to gain an understanding of its weaknesses before going in for the kill? No? Didn't think so.

DOMESTIC DOGS

BEST PET
They're cute and lovable. They'll lick your face when you've had a bad day. This entire book is about them. Need we say more?

A HAIRY HISTORY

WHAT WE KNOW

Recent DNA (also known as the nitty-gritty genetic coding of each and every animal on Earth—serious business) evidence indicates that domestic dogs are, in fact, direct descendants of gray wolves.

THE HISTORY OF DOGS COULD
BE SEPARATED INTO TWO CATEGORIES: WHAT WE
know for sure, and what we think we know (but haven't proven yet).

WHAT WE *THINK* WE KNOW

Most scientists believe that humans began domesticating wolves about 15,000 to 20,000 years ago when we first began living together in communities (as opposed to our hunter-gatherer ancestors who flew solo). It probably all started when wolves, as scavengers, began hanging out on the outskirts of settlements looking for scraps of food and eating our trash. In turn, the people probably appreciated this waste-removal system—there were no garbage trucks, after all—and let them hang around.

LET'S GET TOGETHER

Over time, as humans and wolves became accustomed to each other, people probably saw that wolves were useful for many things, such as getting rid of trash, killing rats and other vermin, alerting the village to danger, and keeping out unwanted carnivores—you know, stuff that dogs are good at. Wolves probably started making their homes in the town, closer to humans, instead of living on the edge of town. At some point, humans began to make use of wolves in their daily lives by hunting with them and keeping them around the house for protection.

BREEDS ARE BORN

Pretty soon, humans were breeding canines, meaning they put them together with a mate to have a litter of pups that humans would raise. Over time, humans would breed dogs specifically for what they needed from them. If they wanted strong hunters, they would breed the dogs with the strongest hunting abilities. If they needed herders, they would breed the dog with the strongest herding instinct. Dog appearances began to differ based on this sort of selective breeding. Their sizes, shapes, coats, and abilities all became increasingly varied. This happened over and over, for thousands of years and . . . voila! Today there are schnauzers, terriers, sheepdogs, and up to 397 other breeds—too many to list here.

THE OTHER THEORY

Of course, that's what we *think* we know. A handful of scientists disagree—they believe dogs evolved from wolves more than 150,000 years ago, which would mean they were not domesticated by humans at all! In fact, the oldest known domestic dog fossil is also debated. Some scientists claim it's the 14,000-year-old fossil found in a Swiss cave. Others think it's the 31,700-year-old fossil discovered more than a century ago in a cave in Belgium. Maybe one day you can settle the scientist smackdown!

PREHISTORIC PUPS

Since the beginning of pets, there has been one great debate: dogs versus cats. Which one is more lovable? Which one is smarter? Which one makes a better pet? But if you dig deep enough, you'll see that they weren't always as different as they are now. In fact, they weren't different at all!

More than 50 million years ago—even before *Eucyon Davisi*, canids (dogs) and felids (cats) lived together (literally!) in the form of one mammal called *Miacis*, which is Greek for "mother animal." Not only that, but many scientists believe bears, raccoons, and weasels came from *Miacis* as well. That certainly is a mother of a mammal!

PAW PRINT THE OLDEST DOMESTIC DOG EVER RECORDED LIVED FOR 29 YEARS AND 5 MONTHS.

WOLVES

IT'S LATE AT NIGHT.
THE SKY IS BLACK, EXCEPT FOR THE LIGHT OF THE FULL MOON. WIND HOWLS THROUGH
the trees. You listen closer . . . the sound gets louder. And louder. More howls now. It's not the wind . . . it's . . . wolves! Run for your life!

Sound familiar? That's probably because you've seen it in movies a dozen times. Relax. Wolves are nothing to be afraid of. In fact, now you know wolves are just the wild cousins of that furry little friend you've got curled up by your feet. So why are people afraid of them? The answer is probably that they don't know much about them. Here's what you need to know to be an expert in the ways of the wolf.

PAW PRINT JUST LIKE A GROUP OF DOGS WHEN THEY BARK, WHEN ONE WOLF HOWLS, OTHERS JOIN IN.

PART OF THE PACK

Like our domesticated pups, wolves are predators that spend most of their time hunting, eating, and sleeping. Unlike our pups, a wolf's life is centered around its pack. Wolf packs consist of at least 8 or 9 animals, though some packs may be as large as 20 or even 30 wolves. They are kind of like a human family in that they watch out and take care of each other.

In a wolf pack, the alpha male and alpha female are the bosses—kind of like parents. They are usually the largest, strongest, and oldest wolves in the pack, and they are not shy about letting other wolves know they are in charge. The alpha wolves are the only wolves in the pack that have pups, though other wolves may pitch in to help raise them.

COMMUNICATION IS KEY

One of the reasons our pet dogs might be so expressive is because, in the pack, wolves need to communicate with one another to survive. They do this through sound, smell, body language, and even facial expressions. And that howling? Well, scientists aren't exactly sure why they do that, though many believe they howl for different reasons. A lone wolf may howl to call out to its pack. A wolf pack may howl territory warnings to other packs. Other scientists think they might just howl out of excitement, or to mark the start of a hunt.

IT'S A DOG-EAT-DEER WORLD

Packs are very important for a number of reasons, but perhaps the most important is hunting. Wolves are not picky eaters, and they will eat a rabbit or rodent if it comes their way, but what they really want is the big stuff like elk, moose, or deer. Wolves are powerful, but taking down prey twice your size requires a group effort. The alpha wolves organize the hunt, and eat first. All of the other wolves get leftovers. Wolves are not delicate eaters, and because food is not always available, they eat as much as they can when they can. A single wolf may eat 20 pounds (9.1 kg) of food at one time.

NO TRESPASSING

One pack will rule an area of land called a territory, where they live and hunt. Territories may be as small as 20 miles (32.2 km), or as large as 1,000 miles (1,609 km). Wolves mark their territory by spreading their scent on rocks, trees, and other landmarks in the area. They might do this by rubbing against things, or peeing on them. That means, no other wolves allowed.

EXPLORER'S CORNER

While I've never had any wild wolves at the shelter, I have seen a few wolf hybrids (a mix of a wolf and domestic dog). They are not legal in most states. The differences are noticeable. Usually they look like wolves mixed with Lab or shepherd. They have more rigid body posture, and their eyes are not as open. They don't wag their tails as much, and they're not as approachable. A wolf hybrid's behavior is always unpredictable because it has so much of its wild roots. Wolves are wonderful creatures, but probably not so great to have around the house.

THE NOT-SO-SCARY TRUTH

People have been conditioned to think of wolves as scary predators out to harm humans. The truth is, you're not really their favorite food. Like most animals in the wild, they just want to be left alone. If you don't bother wolves, chances are, they won't bother you.

A WILD WORLD OF CANIDS

MOST SCIENTISTS BELIEVE THERE ARE THREE SPECIES OF WOLVES: gray, red, and Ethiopian. But in the gray wolf species alone, there are dozens and dozens of subspecies, as is the case with most members of the family Canidae. In fact, there are so many species and sub- species of wild canines that you might get bored reading about all of them, so here are a few of our favorite puppy picks.

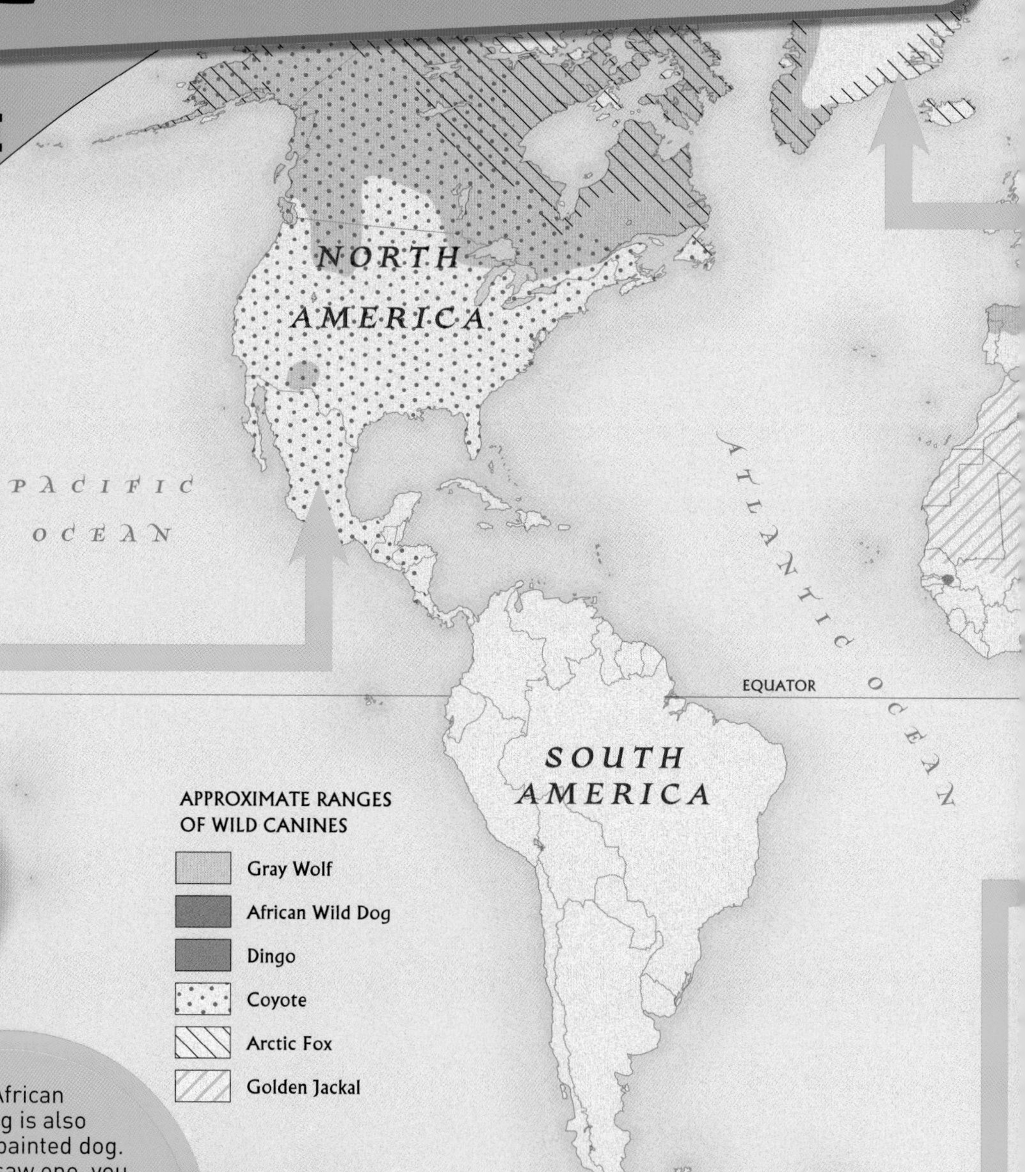

NORTH AMERICA

PACIFIC OCEAN

ATLANTIC OCEAN

EQUATOR

SOUTH AMERICA

APPROXIMATE RANGES OF WILD CANINES

- Gray Wolf
- African Wild Dog
- Dingo
- Coyote
- Arctic Fox
- Golden Jackal

COYOTE
Canis latrans

Unlike wolves, coyotes are not endangered. In fact, many scientists think their population is at an all-time high. Coyotes used to roam the prairies and grasslands of North America, but now they mostly live in the mountains or forests. They can be found as far south as Central America.

The African wild dog is also called the painted dog. And if you saw one, you would know why. Their coat is covered in splotches of black, white, red, and tan that make them look like a work of art! African wild dogs mostly roam the open plains of sub-Saharan Africa.

AFRICAN WILD DOG
Lycaon pictus

Gray wolves, the ancestors of dogs, are the largest and most common wolf. There are more than 30 subspecies of gray wolf, and they are not just gray. They come in red, brown, white, and black, too! Gray wolves can be found in different places all over the world.

GRAY WOLF
Canis lupus

ARCTIC FOX
Vulpes lagopus

These snow-white pups may look like cuddly lapdogs, but they are among the hardiest animals on Earth. Their fluffy coats not only serve as camouflage so they blend in to their icy setting, but also help them survive in the frozen Arctic tundra environment, where temperatures can reach minus 58°F (-50°C)!

GOLDEN JACKAL
Canis aureus

Scientists think the golden jackal is more closely related to the gray wolf than to other jackal species. Much smaller than a wolf in size, it has been known to follow larger prey in search of their leftovers. The golden jackal has a large area of distribution, covering parts of Africa, Europe, and Asia.

SCALE AT THE EQUATOR

0 ————————— 2,000 miles

0 ————————— 2,000 kilometers

DISAPPEARING WOLVES

Wolves were once prominent on every continent except Antarctica, but their numbers have decreased significantly over the past 200 years. There are a couple of contributing factors, but the main reason is overhunting. While wolves do not pose much of a threat to humans, they do attack farm animals. Because of this, humans have killed millions of wolves. The second reason is that their natural habitat is decreasing as humans populate more of the land. But there is good news! Many organizations have taken notice of the dwindling population of wolves and stepped in to help. You can help too by learning all you can about wolves and telling your friends. The more we know, the better able we are to protect them.

DINGO
Canis lupus dingo

The dingo is a wild dog that roams the open plains of Australia, mostly in the remote areas of the outback. It is also found in parts of Southeast Asia. In Australia, there are so many dingoes that a fence was erected to protect local livestock from these predators. In Asia, dingoes are found near villages where people have been known to give them food and shelter.

DOG COMPARISONS

THE NOSE KNOWS

YOU AND YOUR

DOG DO EVERYTHING TOGETHER. YOU WAKE up, eat, and play together . . . you even sleep in the same bed! Your dog is just like a brother or a sister. Right? Well, maybe. But no matter how much time you spend with each other, there will always be a few big differences between man and mutt.

Dogs have about 220 million scent cells. That's about 40 times more than humans, who only have 5 million. Also, the part of the brain that identifies these scents is 40 percent larger in dogs than it is in people. Scientists think this means a dog can identify smells 1,000 to 10,000 times better than a human can, which is why they use scent just as we use sight: It's where they get most of their information.

PAW PRINT SCIENTISTS THINK DOGS' ABILITY TO TASTE WATER MIGHT BE NATURE'S WAY OF MAKING THEIR ANCESTORS SEEK WATER IN THE WILD BECAUSE THEIR BODIES NEED IT TO SURVIVE.

SEE THE DIFFERENCE?

There is a common myth that dogs can't see color. They do, they just have fewer cone receptors than humans (that's the technical term for the things in your eye that respond to light and decipher colors). So, where humans see the primary colors red, yellow, and blue, dogs only see yellow and blue. Which means their sense of color is much duller than ours, and they cannot judge distance well.

HEIGHTENED HEARING

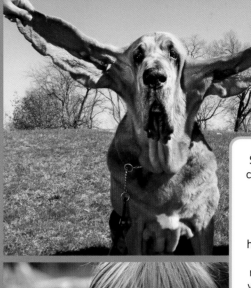

Sound is measured in a unit called a hertz. The higher the number of hertz, the more high-pitched the sound. Humans can hear sounds up to 23,000 Hz. Dogs can hear sounds up to 45,000 Hz. That means that your dog may respond to sounds that you don't hear at all! Also, at the high and low end of our hearing spectrum, sounds must be much louder for humans to hear them than for dogs, so your pup might hear an ambulance siren way before you do.

TERRIBLE TASTE

In terms of survival, taste is very important. In the wild if something tastes bad, it might be dangerous to eat. But humans still win this one. We have about 9,000 taste buds and our furry friends only have 1,700.

Humans respond to four primary tastes: sweet, salty, sour, and bitter. Studies show that dogs respond to the same chemicals we do, with one exception: salt. Humans crave it. Dogs don't. That's because they are carnivores and eat meat. Meat naturally has a lot of salt, so dogs don't need it the way humans do. Dogs make up for their lack of taste buds by having special taste receptors that humans don't have, specifically for tasting fat and water.

These miniature poodles are living in the lap of luxury.

4 FUN WITH DOGS

QUIZ: YOUR PERFECT POOCH

NOW THAT YOU KNOW

EVERYTHING ABOUT THEM, YOU'RE DYING for a dog, right? But there are so many out there, which one should you pick? Take this handy quiz to find out which breed might be your best bud.

1 **What's your favorite thing to do on a Saturday?**
A. Play sports
B. Play video games
C. Read a book
D. Watch a movie
E. Depends on your mood

2 **If you're feeling down, what do you do?**
A. Go for a run
B. Channel surf
C. Do some online research
D. Hang out with a friend
E. All of the above

3 **Your ideal family vacation would be:**
A. Skiing or surfing
B. Lying on a beach
C. Visiting historical sites
D. Going to an amusement park
E. Any of these sound great!

4 **What's your favorite class in school?**
A. Gym
B. Lunch
C. History, Science, English—if it's academic, you'll take it!
D. Music
E. Eh, they're all kind of the same

5 **Which of these names would you most likely choose for a dog?**
A. Chase
B. Marshmallow
C. Thomas Edison
D. Mr. Prickle Pants
E. You wouldn't know until you saw the dog

6 **If school were closed for a snow day, how would you spend the day?**
A. Building a snowfort
B. Chillin' in a snowfort someone else built
C. Inside catching up on homework and drinking cocoa
D. Building snowmen in the likeness of your family
E. Why choose one when you could do them all?

AUSTRALIAN CATTLE DOG

CHIHUAHUA

MASTIFF

PAW PRINT DOGS HAVE SWEAT GLANDS ON THE PADS OF THEIR FEET AND ON THEIR NOSES.

WHAT'S YOUR IDEAL DOG?

IF YOU CHOSE MOSTLY

A's, you need a: **Fit fetcher!**
Look at you, you sporty superstar! Whether it's cross-country or basketball, soccer or tennis, one thing is true—you love to be active! And boy, are you good at it! If it involves running or swimming? Sign you up. So why would your dream dog be any different? You need a dog that will love your active lifestyle just as much as you do.

BREEDS TO CONSIDER?
Australian cattle dog, border collie, Labrador retriever, Dalmatian, Weimaraner, Portuguese water dog, golden retriever

IF YOU CHOSE MOSTLY

B's, you need a: **Mellow mutt!**
You are the Commander of Comfort. The Chief of Chill. The Sergeant of Sofa . . . You get the idea. When it comes to stuff to do, relaxation is on the top of your list. So why get off the couch when it's cold and rainy out, when you could have a dog that's perfectly happy curling up next to you?

BREEDS TO CONSIDER?
English bulldog, pug, bullmastiff, Chihuahua, Bernese mountain dog, greyhound

IF YOU CHOSE MOSTLY

C's, you need a: **Clever canine!**
Pop quiz, Einstein: What makes honor roll, gets a kick out of homework, and needs a dog just as smart as he or she is? YOU. That's right. You love to learn. Mastering a subject or skill is as big a thrill as scaling a mountain. So why would you settle for a pup that knows how to sit when you could train one to use the toilet? Your perfect pooch would go to the head of the class in no time.

BREEDS TO CONSIDER?
Rottweiler, Jack Russell terrier, papillon, Shetland sheepdog, Doberman pinscher, poodle, German shepherd

IF YOU CHOSE MOSTLY

D's, you need a: **Funny Fido!**
You spend your lunch period practicing stand-up comedy. Your idea of the perfect TV show would star you. You're darn entertaining, and you know it. You need a pup that loves the spotlight as much as you, and is hilarious enough to be your canine warm-up act.

BREEDS TO CONSIDER?
Boston terrier, boxer, dachshund, French bulldog, basset hound, Chinese crested

IF YOU CHOSE MOSTLY

E's, you need a: **Best all-round hound!**
You don't necessarily want a dog that needs to run five hours a day. Or one that refuses to get up off the couch. You need a well-balanced breed that will go with the flow just like you! Want to go on a walk? Grab a leash! Don't feel like it? Take a nap! You and your pup will be the kings and queens of cool and casual.

BREEDS TO CONSIDER?
Yorkshire terrier, beagle, Newfoundland, vizsla, Pembroke Welsh corgi, Saint Bernard, American Staffordshire terrier

BASSET HOUND

DOBERMAN PINSCHER

AMERICAN STAFFORDSHIRE TERRIER

DOGS BY DESIGN

HAVING TROUBLE

DECIDING WHICH OF THE 350–400 breeds of purebred dogs might be right for you? Well, that decision is about to get harder, because there are literally thousands of other types of dogs to choose from as well. They vary in size, shape, appearance, and behavior, but they all have the same name: mutt.

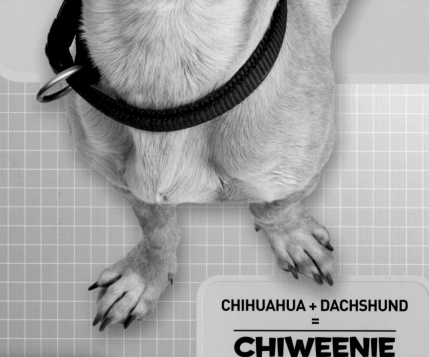

BOXER +
LABRADOR RETRIEVER
=
BOXADOR

CHIHUAHUA + DACHSHUND
=
CHIWEENIE

PAW PRINT   FOR $50,000, SCIENTISTS WILL CLONE (COPY) YOUR DOG.

MIXED-UP MUTTS!

A mutt is any dog that comes from a mix of two or more breeds of dogs—that means they could be a mix of 6, 10, or 50 breeds, depending on their family history. And if you ask any mutt owner, that is fine by them. Mutts are generally as loving and loyal as the purebreds they descended from. Studies show they might even have fewer health problems than their purebred counterparts. Sometimes mutts happen by accident. Sometimes they happen on purpose. But they usually make terrific pets!

GOLDEN RETRIEVER
+
POODLE
=
GOLDENDOODLE

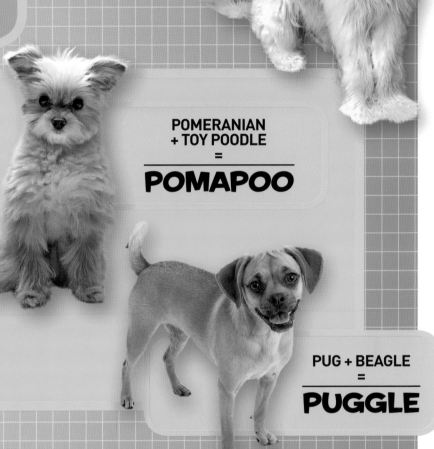

DESIGNER DOGS

Historically, purebred pets have been the most desired dogs. Now there's a new trend afoot that is giving mutts their time to shine: designer dogs. That is, the intentional mixing of two purebred breeds to give one desired outcome. Here are a few of the most popular combinations:

POMERANIAN
+ TOY POODLE
=
POMAPOO

BOSTON
TERRIER
+
PUG
=
BUGG

PUG + BEAGLE
=
PUGGLE

BEAGLE +
BASSET HOUND
=
BAGLE HOUND

DOGGIE DNA

For some mutts, it's easy to pick out purebred features and figure out their furry family tree. For others, there's no telling who their ancestors are! Well, thanks to science it's simple to decipher your mutt from Akita to Yorkshire.

Websites like canineheritage.com offer doggie DNA kits that you can send off in the mail. When the kit arrives at your house, it contains instructions and a cotton swab that you swipe on the inside of your dog's cheek, put in a special tube, and mail back. In two to three weeks . . .Ta-da! You have the full background of your dog.

DNA tests are not free, and your dog might be a little freaked out by the cotton swab, so best to ask your parent's permission before you try this one at home.

CANINE HALL OF FAME

FROM RIN TIN TIN

TO TOTO, LASSIE TO GOOFY, DOGS real and imaginary have graced the silver screen for a hundred years, and the printed page for centuries before that. These are some of our most famous four-legged friends.

Name: BO
Breed: Portuguese water dog
Claim to Fame: First pup
The Scoop: Before he entered office, President Barack Obama promised his daughters, Sasha and Malia, that the White House would soon be getting an extra resident of the furry, slobbery kind. The search was on! What kind of dog would the Obamas get? Letters of suggestion poured in. The news covered it nightly. Soon, the President made good on his promise. Bo moved into the White House on April 14, 2009.

Name: RIN TIN TIN
Breed: German shepherd
Claim to Fame: The first dog movie star
The Scoop: Rin Tin Tin was rescued from the frontline trenches in France during World War I. He was brought to the United States by Lee Duncan, an American pilot, who trained and raised the pup as his own. Rin Tin Tin starred in his first movie in 1922, and went on to make 25 more films. At the height of his career, he was a huge movie star, receiving 10,000 fan letters a week and earning roughly five million dollars a year.

PAW PRINT   RIN TIN TIN SAVED WARNER BROTHERS STUDIOS FROM FINANCIAL RUIN.

Name: BERRY
Breed: German shepherd
Claim to Fame: Starred as Padfoot in the *Harry Potter* movies
The Scoop: Berry played Sirius Black's "animagus" form of the black dog that would watch over Harry from the shadows and acted as his protector. In real life, Berry is a sweet, lovable, stunt dog who is now living a quiet life in retirement. In 2011, Berry's owner was no longer able to take care of him and gave him to a German shepherd rescue in the United Kingdom, which promptly found him a happy forever home.

HOW TO MAKE PUPPY PAPER

You'll need:

Nontoxic water-based paint

Soap, water, and old rags (to clean up)

Banner paper or construction paper

A dog that will cooperate

A sponge brush

1 Go outside. Do not attempt this indoors.

2 Dip the sponge brush into the paint of your choice, and dab all over the bottom of your dog's paws.

3 Lay the paper out across a hard surface, so that it won't tear when your pup walks across it.

4 Have your dog walk, run, or jump across the paper, being sure to leave his mark behind.

5 Wash your dog's paws while allowing the paper to dry completely.

6 Use to decorate, wrap presents, make cards . . . anything you want!

Name: TERRY
Breed: Cairn terrier
Claim to Fame: Played Toto in the movie *The Wizard of Oz*
The Scoop: Terry the cairn terrier actually appeared in 13 different films in her lifetime, but was most famous for her role as Toto. During production, a guard accidentally stepped on Terry's foot and broke it, so some of the filming had to be done by a dog double. Terry's owner was paid $125 a week while on the set, which was $75 more than some of the human actors were paid. Terry passed away in 1945, but it wasn't until 2011 that a permanent memorial was established for her at the Hollywood Forever Cemetery in Los Angeles.

Name: DUG
Breed: "Golden Mutt"
Claim to Fame: Star of Disney's *Up!*
The Scoop: Dug stars as the talking mutt who just wants to be loved. He is totally devoted to his master and dislikes squirrels. Bob Peterson, the animator who voiced Dug, says his inspiration for the character was a combination of all the dogs he ever owned. Also, Dug's famous line, "I have just met you, and I love you," came from something a camper said to Peterson when he was a camp counselor in college.

DOGS WITH JOBS

DOES YOUR PUP HAVE THE STUFF?

If your dog isn't able to sniff out a stranded sea turtle or win a Nobel Peace Prize, don't be too hard on him. Most dogs can't, but there is another test to see if your dog can be a Superdog.

Schutzhund, which means "protection dog," is a sport that was invented in Germany to test whether or not individual German shepherds possessed the "ability to work." Today, it is a popular method in training police dogs for active duty, and dogs of all breeds, shapes, and sizes compete. The competition consists of three areas: obedience, tracking, and protection. Dogs must pass all three areas in one trial to be awarded the Schutzhund title. There are many local Schutzhund chapters—a little research will help to find one near you!

PAW PRINT IT COSTS $60,000 TO TRAIN A NAVY SEAL DOG.

MOST DOGS THESE DAYS

HAVE A VERY IMPORTANT JOB: BRINGING JOY INTO THE LIVES OF THEIR FAMILIES. BUT FOR thousands of dogs around the world, there is actual difficult and sometimes dangerous work to be done. Check out these incredible dogs that are saving lives every day!

SKY THE "WING DOG"

You may not think of a dog chasing birds as all that important, but it is for the young border collie Sky when he's on a mission. Sky works at Southwest International Airport in Fort Myers, Florida, and his job is simple: keep the birds away. Large birds, like Canada geese, choose airfields all over the world as ideal resting stops on their migrations north and south. Why? Airfields are fenced in, so there are no natural predators. But the birds pose a threat to planes mid-landing or during takeoff, because if the plane strikes a bird in a certain way, it can lose power in the engines. It's bad for the bird, and it's bad for the people on board. But birds are not genetically encoded to be afraid of people or noisy planes, so what's the airport to do? Hire a dog. Canines all over the country are finding work as "wing dogs," and the number of bird strikes has decreased significantly. The airports are thankful, and the dogs are having a great time at work.

ACTIVE DUTY DOGS

Dogs have been aiding soldiers in combat since ancient times. They were vital to the war effort during World Wars I and II, so much so that they were inducted into the United States Army in 1942. Since then, they have been employed in all facets of the military, including the United States Air Force. That's right! There are even puppy paratroopers that jump out of helicopters and planes for important missions on the ground. It has been reported that dogs were key to the success of the military during their recent missions in Afghanistan and Iraq, with as many as 2,700 canines reporting for active duty in early 2010.

DOGGIE DOCTORS

A dog's nose is useful for sniffing out many things—bombs and drugs are the most common uses for canines on call—but cancer? It's true! Recent research shows that dogs might actually be able to sniff out the deadly disease that up until now has stumped scientists. Researchers in Germany tested four dogs, including two German shepherds, an Australian shepherd, and a Labrador retriever, to see if the dogs could correctly identify patients with lung cancer versus healthy patients by smelling samples of their breath. The results were impressive: The dogs identified cancer correctly in 71 of the 100 patients who had it. They were given a second test of 400 patients, and they only misidentified 7 percent. Lung cancer is easier to treat if it is diagnosed early, but it is difficult to detect. With the help of these dynamic dogs, who knows how many lives can be saved?

CONSERVATION CANINES

These playful pups are trained to focus their high-energy personalities on a single mission: finding animal poop. Why? Scientists use genetic, dietary, and behavioral information found in an animal's poop to track endangered species! Because of a dog's endless urge to play and its ability to tread on turf that humans can't, these dogs have the ability to find valuable information at a speed and efficiency unmatched by other scientific equipment. Some dogs are even being used to track endangered tigers in Cambodia!

PHOTO FINISH

BEHIND THE SHOT WITH DR. GARY WEITZMAN

BETTY CROCKER AND JAKE ARE MY TWO

rescue dogs. They were both brought to the Washington Animal Rescue League (WARL) a number of years ago, and when I met them, I knew they were meant for me.

Jake is a three-legged German shepherd. In fact, he's my third dog who has had only three legs! The police brought Jake to the shelter when he was only three months old. His former owner had hurt him, and this little puppy was in need of medical attention and lots of love. Jake's hind leg was broken, and he had bruises around his head. We were able to take care of the bruises, but his leg was in bad shape. We tried to repair it, but the damage was too great—our only option was to amputate. But once his surgery was over and we nursed him back to health, Jake was a happy puppy, ready for a happy home! Today he is a healthy and playful German shepherd who loves to run around. And no one who knows him ever thinks of him

as "the 3-legged dog." I don't even think he knows it!

My other dog is a pit bull mix. We call her Betty, but her full name is "Betty Crocker" because she is so sweet. I got Betty after Jake's "sister" Lucy passed away. I knew Jake would need a companion because he was still a very active three-year-old dog.

Betty came to the WARL shelter from rural West Virginia with her six brothers and sisters. All of her siblings are now about twice her size and they're all jet black with big, boxy heads. As you can see from the picture, Betty looks nothing like that! She was the only one in the litter with a brindle, or patterned, coat. The hospital manager who was taking care of Betty decided to bring her to my office to meet Jake for a play date. They got along wonderfully and became best friends. The rest is history. Betty is one of the friendliest, happiest dogs I have ever seen, and she's a great pit bull ambassador to show the world what great dogs pit bulls can be.

TO THE RESCUE!

NOW THAT YOU KNOW ALL
THERE IS TO KNOW ABOUT DOGS, YOU'LL PROBABLY AGREE THAT THEY ARE THE ULTIMATE PET.
So why are so many dogs in need of help?

The answer is simple. There are too many of them. Sadly, humans are to blame. A lot of people breed dogs because there is money to be made by selling them. Breeding is not always a bad thing, but it's not always done responsibly. Responsible breeders have litters in clean, healthy, controlled environments. They do not overbreed their dogs, which is dangerous to the mother and causes overpopulation. They are not churning out puppies for the sake of profit. But some places, called puppy mills, do just that. They keep adult dogs in an unsafe, unhealthy environment, and they overproduce puppies in the same poor conditions. They get rid of puppies with any sort of defect (such as a color that's not ideal) by releasing them into the wild, or even worse. Many puppies do not survive.

Other people simply have pets that they do not spay or neuter. Some dogs have litters by accident, and that also adds to the population of homeless animals.

Shelters such as the Washington Animal Rescue League (WARL) exist to help these animals by taking in puppies and adult dogs that have been rescued from illegal puppy mills or strays from off the street. They also take dogs of any age that people surrender. Many people think getting a dog will be fun because dogs are cute and playful. They do not realize the amount of work involved. Dogs can be hyper, messy, loud, or even aggressive. Many people simply bite off more than they can chew.

At WARL, dogs and cats are given a fresh start. They receive medical care and behavioral training that most of the animals have never had. They are loved and treated with care, so that they understand what it is like to have a human connection. The veterinarians, trainers, adoption coordinators, and volunteers heal them enough to get them into good homes, where they can live with forever families.

If you would like to help, visit www.warl.org for more information.

HOW YOU CAN HELP

IF YOUR PARENTS ARE OPEN TO GETTING a dog, you can help by adopting one. There are so many dogs in shelters that need homes, and adoption is a great way to help out. But you should remember that it is a lot of work. The average lifespan of a dog is about 14 years, and that's a long commitment.

If your parents don't love the idea of a dog in the house, you can still get involved. Most shelters have great education programs. You can learn all about dogs and play with shelter pups, and many places let volunteers help them take care of the dogs. Other ideas might be to raise awareness about the shelter and to raise money from a bake sale, car wash, or maybe even a dog-walking business. Some shelters even allow you to throw birthday parties at their facilities. The ideas are endless! No matter what you do to help, in big ways or small, you are making a difference in the lives of these amazing animals.

A Lab-husky mix and a Labrador retriever enjoy a hike through the park on a warm spring day.

AN INTERACTIVE GLOSSARY

A fluffy Pomeranian pup poses for the camera. Pomeranians originally came from an area called Pomerania, in present-day Germany and Poland.

THESE WORDS ARE COMMONLY
USED AMONG DOG EXPERTS. USE THE GLOSSARY

to learn what each word means and visit the pages listed to see the word used in context. Then test your dog IQ!

1. Agility
The ability to move quickly and easily
(PAGE 27)

What are agility competitions designed to test?
a. How high a dog can jump
b. How fast a dog can run
c. How well a dog can follow commands
d. How well a dog can dig in dirt

2. Ancestor
A related, earlier form of present-day animals
(PAGES 17, 34, 36-37, 40)

What is the ancestor of the domestic dog?
a. Gray wolf
b. Dingo
c. Coyote
d. Fox

3. Behavior
The way in which living things act in response to their environment
(PAGES 6, 17)

A common dog behavior is barking. Why do dogs bark?
a. To call their friends
b. To mark the start of a hunt
c. Because humans bred it into them as the first alarm system
d. To hear their echo

4. Carnivore
An animal that eats the flesh of other animals
(PAGES 25, 37, 43)

What features help wild dogs catch their meal?
a. A soft, fluffy coat
b. Sharp, pointy teeth
c. A cold, wet nose
d. A long tail

5. Demeanor
Outward behavior toward others
(PAGE 28)

When a dog's ears are up and its tail is wagging, what is its demeanor?
a. Scared
b. Anxious
c. Aggressive
d. Friendly

6. Dominant
Being commanding over others
(PAGES 28, 39)

In a wolf pack, the dominant male and female are called the_____.
a. Alpha wolves
b. Top dogs
c. Super canines
d. Rulers

7. Evolve
To develop and change over time
(PAGES 12, 34, 37)

Domestic dogs evolved into about how many different breeds?
a. 10-20
b. 100-200
c. 75-300
d. 350-400

8. Genetics
A branch of biology that studies the genes and characteristics of living things
(PAGES 25, 34, 36, 53)

Genetic evidence shows what about domestic dogs?
a. They can do amazing tricks.
b. They make great pets.
c. They were bred by humans.
d. They are descended from wolves.

9. Instinct
A natural impulse
(PAGES 6, 14, 16-17, 37)

Which of the following do dogs do because it's part of their instincts?
a. Chase things
b. Hide food
c. Roll in dead stuff
d. All of the above

10. Mammal
A warm-blooded animal whose young feed on milk that is produced by the mother
(PAGES 34-35, 37)

Which of the following prehistoric animals was a mammal?
a. *Tyrannosaurus Rex*
b. *Miacis*
c. Pterodactyl
d. *Triceratops*

11. Obedience
Ability of a dog to follow and obey directions
(PAGES 13, 27, 52)

Obedience is a skill that all good _____must have.
a. Water dogs
b. Retrievers
c. Service dogs
d. Lapdogs

12. Predator
An animal that hunts and eats other animals
(PAGES 10, 17, 39, 53)

Which of the following is a predator most likely to eat?
a. Corn
b. Grass
c. Berries
d. Deer

13. Purebred
Dogs that are born to members of the same breed
(PAGES 48-49)

Which of the following dogs is purebred?
a. English bulldog
b. Puggle
c. Mutt
d. Boxador

14. Scavenger
An animal that feeds on whatever dead creatures it can find
(PAGES 17, 25, 36)

What behavior in dogs is most likely the result of their scavenger ancestors?
a. Fetching
b. Hiding food
c. Rolling in dead things
d. Catching a Frisbee

15. Submissive
An animal that is passive and obedient to other animals
(PAGE 28)

A submissive dog will most likely do what?
a. Jump up and lick your face
b. Arch its back and bark ferociously
c. Roll over and reveal its tummy
d. Bare its teeth and growl

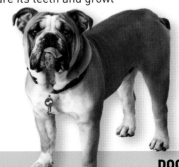

FIND OUT MORE

BOOKS

A Boy and His Dog: The Ultimate Handbook for Every Boy Who Cares for His Dog
Cynthia Copeland
Applesauce Press, 2009.

Face to Face With Wolves
Jim Brandenburg
National Geographic Children's Books, 2008.

National Geographic Readers: Cats vs. Dogs
Elizabeth Carney
National Geographic Children's Books, 2011.

National Geographic Readers: Wolves
Laura Marsh
National Geographic Children's Books, 2012.

The Complete Dog Book for Kids
American Kennel Club, 1996.

MOVIES TO WATCH

My Dog: An Unconditional Love Story
New Video, 2009

Nature: Dogs That Changed the World
Questar, 2007

NOVA: Dogs and More Dogs
PBS, 2004

NOVA: Dogs Decoded
PBS, 2010

Through a Dog's Eyes
PBS, 2010

WEBSITES

National Geographic Kids
animals.nationalgeographic.com/animals/mammals/domestic-dog
animals.nationalgeographic.com/animals/mammals/wolf
kids.nationalgeographic.com/kids/photos/dogs-with-jobs
kids.nationalgeographic.com/kids/photos/gallery/dogs

Animal Planet
animal.discovery.com/tv/dogs-101

American Kennel Club
www.akc.org

Washington Animal Rescue League
www.warl.org

PLACES TO VISIT

The American Kennel Club Museum of the Dog in St. Louis, Missouri, is a great place to learn more about man's best friend!
www.museumofthedog.org

If you're interested in visiting a dog shelter to adopt, foster, or volunteer, check out the ASPCA website to find one near you!
www.aspca.org/adoption/shelters/

Baker, a shepherd border collie mix and pet of National Geographic employee Kate Renner, was voted NG's cutest dog during "Dog-Off," a society-wide photo contest. Facing stiff competition, Baker won the most votes of the 100-plus supercute contestants, earning him a spot in this book.

Photo Credits
Cover, Martin D. Beebee; Back cover, Rechitan Sorin/Shutterstock; Front flap, top to bottom: Eric Isselée/Shutterstock, Lusoimages/Shutterstock, Chris Johns/National Geographic Stock, Senior Airman Elizabeth Rissmiller/U.S. Air Force; Back flap, Lori Epstein/National Geographic Stock, Courtesy of Dr. Gary Weitzman

1, John Crongeyer/National Geographic My Shot; 2-3, AnetaPics/Shutterstock; 5, David Joel/Photographer's Choice RF/Getty Images; 6 (left), Jason Tharp;6 (center), courtesy Dr. Gary Weitzman; 7, Michael Gatlin/National Geographic My Shot; 8-9, cynoclub/Shutterstock; 10, Lisa Vanderhoop/National Geographic My Shot; 11, Rob Hainer/Shutterstock; 12 (left), Eric Isselée/Shutterstock; 12 (center), Eric Isselée/Shutterstock; 12 (right), Lisa A. Svara/Shutterstock; 13 (top left), Nikolai Tsvetkov/Shutterstock; 13 (left center), Eric Isselée/Shutterstock; 13 (right), Christine Tripp/iStockphoto; 13 (bottom left), Trinity Mirror/Mirrorpix/Alamy; 14 (top left), Eric Isselée/Shutterstock; 14 (bottom left), Julia Remezova/Shutterstock; 14 (right), Julia Remezova/Shutterstock; 15 (top), gillmar/Shutterstock; 15 (left), Eric Isselée/Shutterstock; 15 (center), Erik Lam/Shutterstock; 15 (right), Dancestrokes/Shutterstock; 16, Denis Babenko/Shutterstock; 17 (top right), Kevin,Chen/Shutterstock; 17 (top left), Kimberly Hall/Shutterstock; 17 (bottom right), Digital Vision; 17 (bottom left), Renee Stockdale/Kimball Stock; 18 (inset left), Jason Tharp;18 (inset bottom), Bork/Shutterstock; 18-19, Henri Simon Faure/iStockphoto; 20-21, Mackland/Shutterstock; 22 (top), Igumnova Irina/Shutterstock; 22 (bottom), Stephen Coburn/Shutterstock; 23 (top), Joel Sartore/National Geographic Stock; 23 (bottom left), Eloisa Pavon/National Geographic My Shot; 23 (bottom center), Jason Tharp23 (bottom right), courtesy Barbara Pinette; 24 (left), Traci Scarpinato/National Geographic My Shot; 24 (right), courtesy Lucie McNeil; 25 (left), Nikola Brankovic/National Geographic My Shot; 25 (top right), blanche/Shutterstock; 25 (bottom right), Terekhov Igor/Shutterstock; 26, vgm/Shutterstock; 27 (top left), Andraž Cerar/Shutterstock; 27 (top right), Ron Armstrong/Flickr RF/Getty Images; 27 (bottom), Dennis Donohue/Shutterstock; 28 (A), Andrii Muzyka/Shutterstock; 28 (B), Onur ERSIN/Shutterstock; 28 (C), Nejron Photo/Shutterstock; 28 (D), Marina Jay/Shutterstock; 28 (E), Valeriy Lebedev/Shutterstock; 28 (F), Eric Isselée/Shutterstock; 28 (G), 26kot/Shutterstock; 28 (H), Erik Lam/Shutterstock; 28 (I), Eric Isselée/Shutterstock; 28 (J), Marina Jay/Shutterstock; 28 (K), Erik Lam/Shutterstock; 29 (top), PM Images/Iconica/Getty Images; 29 (bottom left), Poulsons Photography/Shutterstock; 29 (bottom right), ZenShui/Sigrid Olsson/PhotoAlto/Getty Images; 30 (top left), Photodisc/Digital Vision; 30 (top right), Kari Herer/National Geographic My Shot; 30 (bottom right), courtesy Champ Harms; 30 (bottom center), Nikolai Tsvetkov/Shutterstock; 30 (bottom left), Kyle Brent/National Geographic My Shot; 31 (top left), Joy Brown/Shutterstock; 31 (top right), Kristin Halliwill/National Geographic My Shot; 31 (center), Adithep Chokrattanakan/Shutterstock; 31 (bottom left), courtesy Edwin Sherman; 31 (bottom right), Patti Waddell/National Geographic My Shot; 32-33, Klein-Hubert/Kimball Stock; 34 (left), Jeff Mauritzen; 34 (right), Chris Johns/National Geographic Stock; 35 (right), Larry Gambon/National Geographic My Shot; 35 (center), Neale Cousland/Shutterstock; 35 (bottom), Judy Kennamer/Shutterstock; 35 (left), Denis Pepin/Shutterstock; 35 (top), 12qwerty/Shutterstock; 36, Mauricio AntonNational Geographic Stock; 37 (bottom), Jiri Vaclacek/Shutterstock; 37 (top right), Laurie O'Keefe/Photo Researchers Inc./Getty Images; 37 (top left), Sergej Khakimullin/Shutterstock; 38, Tammy Wolfe/iStockphoto; 39 (top left), Nataly Klaric/National Geographic My Shot; 39 (top right), Joel Sartore/National Geographic Stock; 39 (bottom center), Lori Labrecque/Shutterstock; 39 (bottom right), Jason Tharp; 39 (bottom left), Brian Guest/Shutterstock; 40 (center), visceralimage/Shutterstock; 40 (top), Joel Sartore/National Geographic Stock; 40 (bottom), Francois van Heerden/Shutterstock; 41 (top), Jean-Edouard Rozey/Shutterstock; 41 (center), Peter Malsbury/iStockphoto; 41 (bottom), DavidEwingPhotography/Shutterstock; 42 (top), Tracy Hebden/iStockphoto;42 (bottom), picturepartners/Shutterstock; 43 (top left), Boris Mrdja/Shutterstock; 43 (top right), Karine Aigner/NGS Staff; 43 (left center), marinini/Shutterstock; 43 (right center), Elena Rostunova/Shutterstock; 43 (bottom right), gabczi/Shutterstock; 43 (bottom right), Lenkadan/Shutterstock; 44-45, MBWTE Photos/Shutterstock; 45 (top), Cameron Watson/Shutterstock; 46 (bottom), Artem Kursin/Shutterstock; 47 (top), Joy Brown/Shutterstock; 47 (bottom right), Dmitry Kalinovsky/Shutterstock; 47 (bottom left), Zuzule/Shutterstock; 48 (left), Erik Lam/Bigstock; 48 (right), Susan Schmitz/Shutterstock; 49 (bottom left), Gillian Moore/Alamy; 49 (top right), Jennifer Sheets/iStockphoto; 49 (top center), Purestock/Alamy; 49 (right center), Rick's Photography/Shutterstock; 49 (bottom center), Lori Epstein/National Geographic Stock; 50 (left), Christy Bowe/Corbis; 50 (right), Hulton Archive/Getty Images; 51 (top left), courtesy of germanshepherdrescue.co.uk; 51 (bottom left), CinemaPhoto/Corbis; 51 (bottom right), Walt Disney Co./courtesy Everett Collection; 51 (center), Andrija Markovic/Shutterstock; 51 (top center Far left), Petrenko Andriy/Shutterstock; 51 (top center left), Veniamin Kraskov/Shutterstock; 51 (top center), pockygallery/Shutterstock; 51 (top center right), Lobke Peers/Shutterstock; 51, (top far right), Liz Van Steenburgh/Shutterstock; 52, Marcel Jancovic/Shutterstock; 53 (top left), Michel Fortier/Naples Daily News; 53 (bottom left), AP Images/MTI, Barnabas Honeczy; 53 (top right), U.S. Air Force photo/Senior Airman Elizabeth Rissmiller; 53 (bottom right), Center for Conservation Biology, www.ConservationBiology.net; 54, courtesy Dr. Gary Weitzman; 56, courtesy Washington Animal Rescue League; 56-57, courtesy Washington Animal Rescue League; 58-59, Lori Epstein/National Geographic Stock; 60, Sergey Lavrentev/Shutterstock; 61, Deedee Jacobs; 62, courtesy Katharine Renner

For Ellie Jean

With special thanks to Champ Harms, for being funny when I wasn't anymore, Dr. Gary Weitzman and Debbie Duel at the Washington Animal Rescue League for graciously giving me their time and expert opinions, and Bob Barker (the dog, not the man) for being my squishy inspiration. —BB

Prepared by the Book Division
Hector Sierra, *Senior Vice President and General Manager*
Nancy Laties Feresten, *Senior Vice President, Editor in Chief, Children's Books*
Jonathan Halling, Design Director, *Books and Children's Publishing*
Jay Sumner, Director of Photography, *Children's Publishing*
Jennifer Emmett, Editorial Director, *Children's Books*
Eva Absher-Schantz, *Managing Art Director, Children's Publishing*
Carl Mehler, *Director of Maps*
R. Gary Colbert, *Production Director*
Jennifer A. Thornton, *Director of Managing Editorial*

Staff for This Book
Priyanka Lamichhane, *Project Editor*
Eva Absher-Schantz, *Art Director*
Simon Renwick, *Designer*
Lori Epstein, Annette Kiesow, *Illustrations Editors*
Hillary Moloney, *Illustrations Assistant*
Kathryn Robbins, *Design Production Assistant*
Jason Tharp, *Illustrator*
Kate Olesin, *Assistant Editor*
Grace Hill, *Associate Managing Editor*
Joan Gossett, *Production Editor*
Lewis R. Bassford, *Production Manager*
Susan Borke, *Legal and Business Affairs*

Manufacturing and Quality Management
Phillip L. Schlosser, *Senior Vice President*
Chris Brown, *Vice President, NG Book Manufacturing*
George Bounelis, *Vice President, Production Services*
Nicole Elliott, *Manager*
Rachel Faulise, *Manager*
Robert L. Barr, *Manager*

Captions
Page 1: A frisky pup chases a ball into a swimming pool. Some dogs, like this Spaniel breed, are built for swimming.
Pages 2-3: A beagle puppy prances through an open field. These fast and feisty pups were originally bred to hunt rabbits.

Since 1888, the National Geographic Society has funded more than 12,000 research, exploration, and preservation projects around the world. The Society receives funds from National Geographic Partners, LLC, funded in part by your purchase. A portion of the proceeds from this book supports this vital work. To learn more, visit www.natgeo.com/info.

NATIONAL GEOGRAPHIC and Yellow Border Design are trademarks of the National Geographic Society, used under license.

For more information, visit nationalgeographic.com, call 1-877-873-6846, or write to the following address:

National Geographic Partners
1145 17th Street N.W.
Washington, D.C. 20036-4688 U.S.A.

Visit us online at nationalgeographic.com/books

For librarians and teachers: nationalgeographic.com/books/librarians-and-educators

More for kids from National Geographic: natgeokids.com

National Geographic Kids magazine inspires children to explore their world with fun yet educational articles on animals, science, nature, and more. Using fresh storytelling and amazing photography, *Nat Geo Kids* shows kids ages 6 to 14 the fascinating truth about the world—and why they should care.
kids.nationalgeographic.com/subscribe

For rights or permissions inquiries, please contact National Geographic Books Subsidiary Rights: bookrights@natgeo.com

Paperback edition ISBN: 978-1-4263-1024-9
Library edition ISBN: 978-1-4263-1025-6

Printed in Malaysia
20/IVM/6